The Last Gr
RACE
on Earth

Henry Billings and Melissa Billings

Published in association with The Basic Skills Agency

Hodder & Stoughton
A MEMBER OF THE HODDER HEADLINE GROUP

Acknowledgements
Cover: Richard T. Nowitz/Corbis.
Photos: All photos © Corbis.

Orders: please contact Bookpoint Ltd, 39 Milton Park, Abingdon, Oxon OX14 4TD. Telephone: (44) 01235 400414, Fax: (44) 01235 400454. Lines are open from 9.00–6.00, Monday to Saturday, with a 24 hour message answering service. Email address: orders@bookpoint.co.uk

British Library Cataloguing in Publication Data
A catalogue record for this title is available from The British Library

ISBN 0 340 74781 1

Published by Jamestown Publishers,
a division of NTC/Contemporary Publishing Group, Inc.

First published in UK 1999 by Hodder & Stoughton Educational Publishers.
Impression number   10 9 8 7 6 5 4 3 2
Year   2004 2003 2002 2001 2000

Copyright © 1996 by NTC/Contemporary Publishing Group, Inc.

All rights reserved. No part of this publication may be reproduced or transmitted in any form or by any means, electronic or mechanical, including photocopy, recording, or any information storage and retrieval system, without permission in writing from the publisher or under licence from the Copyright Licensing Agency Limited. Further details of such licences (for reprographic reproduction) may be obtained from the Copyright Licensing Agency Limited, of 90 Tottenham Court Road, London W1P 9HE.

Typeset by Fakenham Photosetting Ltd, Fakenham, Norfolk.
Printed in Great Britain for Hodder & Stoughton Educational, a division of Hodder Headline Plc, 338 Euston Road, London NW1 3BH by Redwood Books, Trowbridge, Wiltshire.

The idea of this hard 1,160-mile race
is to get from one end of Alaska
to the other as fast as possible.
The racers travel alone on a sled
pulled by dogs.
That means all the racers
– or mushers as they are called –
push themselves and their dogs
to the limit.

A musher and his dogs.

Sometimes, dogs die along the way.
Mushers know that they, too, might die.
Still, every year people return to run this
'Last Great Race on Earth'.

Mushers can be tall or short,
young or old, men or women.
There is only one thing they cannot be:
cowards.
If they are, they will never survive.

The race begins in the city of Anchorage.
Mushers harness their best 15 or 20
sled dogs.
They jump onto sleds packed with food
and other supplies.
Then they start off.
The race course follows an old route
that used to pass
through Alaska's mining towns.

Racing through Alaska at dawn.

But since the towns are mostly empty now,
the race is one long trek
through the wilderness.
Mushers stop at 18 checkpoints along the way.
Otherwise, they have no contact
with the outside world
until they reach the finishing line in Nome.

With luck, the first hours of the race
go smoothly.
The dogs work well together.
The teams make every twist and turn
in the trail.
The mushers can settle back and enjoy
the snowy silence of the Alaskan land.

Sooner or later, though,
trouble always happens!
The dogs may stumble on rough ground,
cutting their paws
on razor-sharp slivers of ice.
Or they might make a wrong turn.
Then a musher may wander miles off the trail.

Crossing a frozen lake can be dangerous.

Frozen lakes and rivers
can also mean disaster.
If the ice is not thick enough,
the whole team can fall through,
pulling the musher into the icy water.
If that happens,
there is little chance of getting out alive.

Then there are the storms.
Susan Butcher has won the race four times.
She knows all about storms.
She once drove into a blizzard
that left 10-metre high snowdrifts.
In 1985, another winner tried
to push her way through a terrible storm.
It was so bad that for 11 hours
she could not move at all.

The first time one musher tried the race,
he got stuck in a 'killing storm'.

He was a long way from the start
and miles from the nearest checkpoint
when the storm began.
'The wind must have been blowing
70 or 80 miles per hour,' he later wrote.
'I knew it was impossible to do anything
but stop and try to survive.'

He stopped his sled
and climbed into his sleeping bag.
His dogs lay down in the snow,
curling up into tight little balls.
Hours later, after the snow finally stopped,
the musher and his dogs dug themselves out.
Then they carried on with the race.

A musher rests with his dogs.

Even if mushers avoid blizzards,
there is no way to avoid the bitter cold.
Temperatures on the trail can drop
to 50 or 60 degrees below zero.
One musher reported air so cold
it froze the batteries in his torch.
His wooden matches would not light.
In weather like that,
frostbite sets in quickly.
Mushers may arrive at the finish
with frostbitten cheeks, toes or fingers.

Certain parts of the trail
hold special dangers.
Farewell Burn is a 92-mile stretch
of burned-out forest.
The winds that whip through there
blow all the snow away.
So the dogs must pick their way around rocks,
blackened tree stumps and water holes.

One year, Susan Butcher's sled
crashed into a tree
as she raced through the Burn.
She and four of her dogs
were hurt in the accident.

A dog team on the trail.

For some, the toughest part of the trail
is Rainy Pass.
Here, mushers must steer their sleds
along a narrow ledge.
One wrong move can send them
tumbling to their deaths
in a rock-filled canyon.
For others, Happy River is the worst.
To reach it, mushers have to navigate
a 170-metre drop into a canyon.
Then, after crossing the river,
they have to climb out the other side.

All of these dangers
would be hard enough to face
during the day,
after a good night's sleep.
But the mushers travel at night
as well as by day.
And they don't get a good night's sleep.
In fact, they don't get much sleep at all.
They make many short stops
to feed their dogs,
but that is not a time for sleeping.

At checkpoints, they may take a longer break, but even then there is a lot to do.
Mushers need to check their dogs' paws for cuts.
They have to rub their dogs' sore muscles.
They may also need to repair their sleds or fix a broken harness.
Sometimes, mushers have a few hours' sleep at a checkpoint.
But often they just stay for a few minutes, then start off again.

The McGrath checkpoint.

By the middle of the race,
lack of sleep becomes a danger.
Many mushers begin to fall asleep on their sleds.
They have to trust their dogs
to keep running in the right direction.
Some exhausted mushers begin to hallucinate.
They see things that are not there.
Some see imaginary trees or lakes.
One musher saw things like his wife,
a man in a suit, and the seaside.

Storms, lack of sleep
and very cold temperatures
are always part of the race.
But once in a while,
mushers run into something else.
They can come across a crazy moose.
A moose is a big, aggressive deer.
One musher was run over by a moose.
Luckily, he was not badly hurt.
But the same moose
killed a dog in another musher's team.

A bull moose.

Susan Butcher's team was also attacked
one year by a moose.
She tried to scare the moose off with an axe.
But again and again
the animal tried to trample her dogs.
After 20 minutes, another musher came along.
He kept a gun in his sled
and quickly shot the moose.
By then, two of the dogs were dead
and most of the others were hurt.
So Butcher was forced
to drop out of the race.

Dropping out is not something
to be ashamed of.
When things go wrong,
even the best mushers have to give in.
Still, the thrill of crossing
that finishing line
keeps many of them going.

In 1995, one racer set a new speed record
for the race.
He completed the course in just nine days,
two hours and 42 minutes.
To do that, he travelled more than 100 miles
each day.
But even for mushers
who take twice as long to finish,
the Last Great Race on Earth
is still the thrill of a lifetime.

The thrill of finishing the race.